This is a true story detailin
Hoise Birks, an African A
Nouh, a professor, pastor, and evangelist in Mali, West ___
The Holy Spirit inspired this documentation to enlighten and
instruct the reader about Timbuktu as a historical place where
God has raised up witnesses to His power and grace.

Dr. LeRoy Yates
Pastor Emeritus, Westlawn Gospel Chapel
Chicago, Illinois

An awesome narrative! Dr. Birks does a superb job of presenting
the intricacies of ministry in Mali. I felt that I was there
experiencing the entire situation.

Rev. Dr. Virgil Lee Amos
General Director, Ambassadors Fellowship

The friendship forged between Dr. Hoise Birks and Pastor
Nouh epitomizes what can happen when humility and
selflessness meet up with courage and teachability. What began
as an acquaintance with an international leads to a meaningful
relationship and a beneficial partnership that bears much
fruit for the Kingdom as Pastor Nouh and Dr. Birks worked
together over 16 years and across four thousand miles. People
from all walks of life will learn valuable lessons from *Timbuktu
Revisited* from one of the most compassionate men American
soil has produced.

Rev. Robert W. Crummie
Pastor, Mount Calvary Missionary Baptist Church,
College Park, Georgia
President, Carver College, Atlanta, Georgia

"And the things that you have heard from me . . . commit these to faithful men who will be able to teach others also" (II Timothy 2:2).

I thank God for Brother Birks who has been a real mentor to me and many others. His ministry in Mali, West Africa and in countries around the world has been an inspiration to many. May God continue to bless and use him for His glory.

Bro. Julie Prosper
Galilee Gospel Chapel
Corona, New York

I have known the author of *Timbuktu Revisited* since my teen years. His incredible passionate zeal to reach people with the saving Gospel of Jesus Christ in dangerous and remote parts of the Earth is palpable throughout the pages of this book; it inspires me to action. I found myself humbled and yearning for more details of the miraculous work of God in Timbuktu led by the Malian pastor, Rev. Nouh Ag Infa Yattara.

LeRoy Yates, Jr. M.D., FACOG, ABVLM

Rev. Birks' life in the service of the Lord is truly inspiring. It is a testimony of how the Lord can use one believer to touch the hearts and souls of many.

Korey Dowell
Biotech Professional

Timbuktu Revisited

Exploring the Ancient City

Rev. Dr. Hoise Birks

Capstone Publishing Company
Stockbridge, GA

Copyright © 2015 by Rev. Hoise Birks

All rights reserved.

Published in the United States by Capstone Publishing Company
P.O. Box 2171, Stockbridge, GA 30281

Library of Congress Cataloguing-in-Publication Data

Birks, Hoise 1933-
Timbuktu Revisited: Exploring the Ancient City/ Rev. Hoise Birks
p. cm.
Photographs included.
1.Ministry. 2. Missionary Work. 3. Africa. 4. Inspirational Literature. I. Title.
Library of Congress Control Number: 2015946673
ISBN 978-1-4951-6597-9

Printed in the United States of America

Cover Design & Photo Gallery by: Clive Williamson, On Target Communications

Photographs by Hoise Birks

Typesetting by: projectluz.com

Editing by: Mary C. Lewis, MCL Editing, Etc.

Copies of *Timbuktu Revisited* may be ordered at: info@HoiseBirks.com and HBPublishing9@gmail.com

10 9 8 7 6 5 4 3 2 1

First Edition

Dedication

To God's people in Timbuktu:
Continue to persevere in the Lord because
greater is He that is in you
than he that is in the world

Contents

Chapter One

A Godsend and Acceptance 1
*Meeting Pastor Nouh in Philadelphia; resisting and then
accepting God's call to visit Timbuktu*

Chapter Two

First Journey to Mali 11
*Learning about the Belt of Misery and witnessing the Gospel
through live radio; Pastor Nouh's church begins and grows;
pondering missionaries in Third World churches*

Chapter Three

A Liberation Machine and Ancient Knowledge 27
*Americans can help Malians; a profile of Brother Nouh and
a meeting with a man of history; Timbuktu's ancient, rich
manuscripts*

Chapter Four

The Value of Guides 39
*Contrasts between ancient and modern; the critical importance
of water; learned hosts; returning home, newly burdened*

Foreword

Minister Hoise Birks has captured the journey of a man committed to doing God's will in reference to Africa and Timbuktu. This work is very important. The Lord saw fit to unite Hoise Birks and Pastor Nouh on a spiritual track. Despite the risks and dangers from Islamists, Pastor Nouh persevered and became a major voice for the Gospel and a major figure of the Kingdom in his land.

Timbuktu Revisited is about a man of God of African descent going back to our past, and forward to our destiny. It is a glimpse into our historical glory, but also into a challenging present. Hoise Birks and Pastor Nouh are the symbols of hope to a people who have endured so much in the way of persecution and devastation. As one who is very concerned with the destiny of people of African descent, Hoise Birks has caught my passion for the prophecy, history and legacy of what I call the African destiny. He has combined this passion with an unprecedented missionary fervor that comes out clearly in the pages of the book. This is a journey worth reading about. It is a story of two men, one from America, and one from Africa, who represent what I call the dynamic duo and twin towers of power. I am hoping that there will be another installment of the Timbuktu saga. This is true ministry and service at its best to a people of color.

I hope the reader will delve into this book and understand a people of color with a glorious past, a challenging present, and because of men like Dr. Birks and Pastor Nouh, a hopeful future. May they go from Timbuktu Revisited to Timbuktu Revived. I trust that the reader will read *Timbuktu Revisited* and go on the journey with Dr. Birks.

Reverend Clarence Walker, Ph.D.

Preface

When I came back from Timbuktu, I excitedly told everyone about my experiences in that ancient city. I learned much about the people, the history, and the culture. Many were surprised that Timbuktu is an actual place. I was often met with skepticism and many said that they had heard of Timbuktu, but only as a fictitious place. I was continually amazed myself as I walked the dusty streets of a city that is famed for its university, for its wealth in gold, for its prominence as a trade route, and for its manuscripts.

The ancient manuscripts of Timbuktu have played a major role in setting the record straight about knowledge and learning on the African continent. They provide proof that Africa was not the "dark continent", a continent devoid of civilized culture and learning as it was portrayed for years by European scholars. Indeed, the opposite is true. As is clearly shown by the manuscripts, there were many centers of advanced learning in Africa, centers such as the University of Sankore in Timbuktu which were vast repositories of knowledge and learning and to which scholars flocked from both African and European countries. The University of Sankore was in its golden age from the 14th through the 16th centuries while Oxford and

Cambridge in England were in their golden age later, from the 16th through the 19th centuries.

I was fortunate to be introduced to Timbuktu by a native son, Pastor Nouh Yatarra, a brilliant Malian scholar in his own right, who is also a humble servant of Jesus Christ. His heart's desire is that every reader would see that it is the Spirit of God Who works in and through him; Pastor Nouh wants all of the praise and all of the glory to go to God.

Acknowledgments

Many contributed to make this book possible. I have to acknowledge my debt to the brilliant scholar, the late Dr. Ivan Van Sertima whose enthusiasm, encouragement and urging caused me to consider writing about my experiences in Timbuktu. He even suggested a title for the book during one of our many discussions. "You should write about your trips to Timbuktu and call the book *Timbuktu Revisited*," he said. I greatly appreciate Dr. Van Sertima's encouragement.

Others played a vital role in helping me with the book. Thanks to Cris Wanzer at Manuscripts to Go in Geyserville, California for her skillful transcription of my recordings. Thanks to my excellent editor, Mary C. Lewis of MCL Editing, Etc. As always, she does excellent, professional work and is a pleasure to work with. Thanks to the book's gifted graphic designer, Clive Williamson of On Target Communications; Clive makes it a point to give God all the glory for his creative gifts. He is gracious and patient and I deeply appreciate him. Thanks to Paul Lewis of Luz Design for the typesetting.

Thanks to Pastor Nouh for sharing his encyclopedic knowledge of the history and culture of Timbuktu. Most of the facts in the book come from him; it is spellbinding to listen as he reaches into his vast store of knowledge and instantly pulls up facts regarding the history and culture of Timbuktu, and indeed, of all of Mali, West Africa.

I will forever be thankful to my good friend, the late Fouzi Ayoub, who made it possible for me to meet Pastor Nouh. Thanks to Dr. Abdel Kader Haidara, a brilliant Malian scholar, who shared invaluable information regarding Timbuktu's ancient manuscripts. Thanks to the believers in Timbuktu for their loving and gracious hospitality; they warmly embraced me and expressed their gratitude and appreciation for the many ways the believers in the United States showed their care and concern. They were touched and inspired by the fellowship from those so far away. They were thankful for the reading glasses and delighted to receive them. The women danced with joy to celebrate the Liberation Machine (a machine that grinds grain and frees women from the drudgery of pounding grain with a mortar and pestle).

A special thanks goes to the believers at Galilee Gospel Chapel in Queens, New York for their prayers, support and encouragement on each of my three trips to Timbuktu. These believers contributed nearly the entire amount used to purchase the Liberation Machine. Thanks to all who prayed and shared financially (especially during a period of drought in Timbuktu), and to those who donated clothing and shoes for God's people in Timbuktu. Thanks to many friends and partners in other states who undergirded me with their prayers as I went to Timbuktu.

Thanks to my wife Cynthia who helped with the editing and proofreading of the manuscript. Her assistance with many aspects of this project helped to bring it to completion.

Thanks to all who reached out to make *Timbuktu Revisited* possible.

MALI

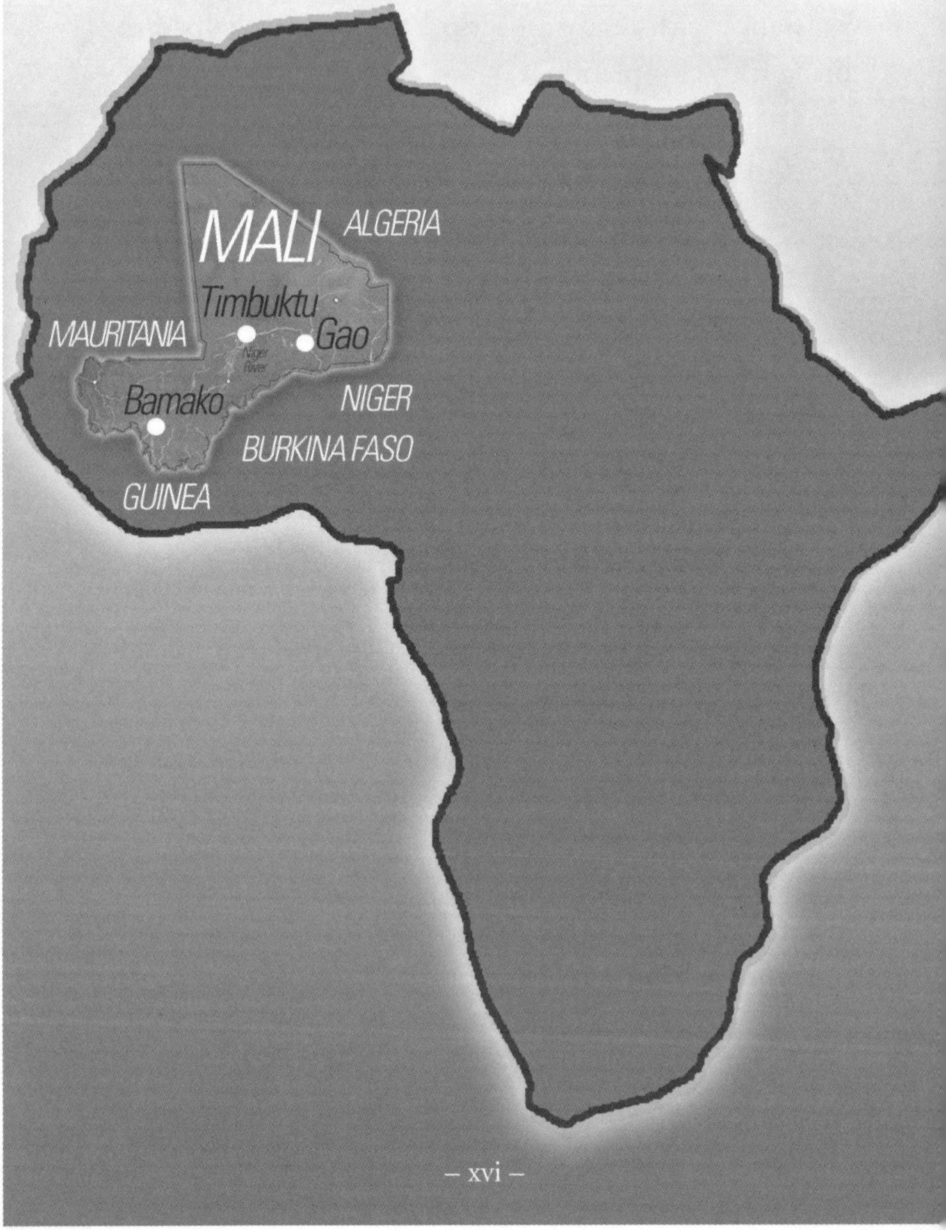

MALI

ALGERIA

Timbuktu

Gao

MAURITANIA

Niger River

NIGER

Bamako

BURKINA FASO

GUINEA

Ancient.

Dusty.

A university town.

Trade in salt, gold, ivory, and slaves.

Distant.

Faraway.

The stuff of myth and legend.

Do these words evoke the mystique
of a place called Timbuktu?

Is there such a place?

Yes, there is. I have been to
Timbuktu and back three times.

Chapter One

A Godsend and Acceptance

I am often amazed by how God has led in my life from the day I accepted Him as my personal Savior in Alaska in 1957. Since then, I have done missionary activity in many other countries with the group known as Operation Mobilization. After my first missionary stint of eight years overseas, I returned to the United States and I continued a close friendship with a brother in England. He invited me from time to time to visit him for ministry in his church and with believers in the school where he works.

In 1997 I was visiting this brother, Fouzi, at his home in Wolverhampton, which is north of London, near Birmingham. As we talked, he mentioned another brother who was studying at Spurgeon's College in London. As I prepared to leave England and return to America, Fouzi encouraged me to leave Wolverhampton a day or two early and stop off in London to meet this dedicated, committed pastor from Gao in Mali, West Africa. Brother Fouzi told

- 1 -

me that this young man, a converted Muslim, would be an encouragement to me and me to him if I would just spend the day in London with him having fellowship. Brother Fouzi and I called him before I left Wolverhampton, and he said that he would be very happy to meet me. Fortunately, I was able to take a train from Wolverhampton to London and this brother picked me up. He graciously took me to his home and it so happened on that particular evening, several students from Spurgeon's College gathered in his home for a prayer meeting. After supper and the prayer meeting, this brother, who I am calling Abraham, told me about another brother, Pastor Nouh, from Timbuktu, also in Mali. Brother Abraham mentioned that Pastor Nouh was studying in America in Philadelphia, and it would be wonderful if I had a chance to talk to him by phone and get to know him and his ministry before he returned to Mali.

I took my flight from London back to New York where I was living at the time. After returning to the United States, I waited a week or two before I called him on the phone and informed him that I received his name from Brother Abraham in London when I passed through; I told him I would love to come and visit him one day. He was living off campus in Philadelphia working on his master's degree in community development. His course in economic development was geared to help him help his people when he returned to his country. I was thinking that since he was a student, he would not have much time for visitors.

I asked Brother Nouh if I could come early some morning when he did not have classes, have lunch with him, spend a little time there, and return to New York the same day. It would take only about two hours by train to get to Philadelphia, so I thought it would be workable. Brother Nouh gave me his address and instructions on how to get to his home by train and bus.

The following weekend I followed his instructions, but somehow I got off the bus maybe one or two stops before I got to his home, and I realized I was a little confused. His home was not in immediate sight, but when I looked down the street, I saw three young boys in the middle of the street beckoning me, about five blocks away. I wasn't sure they were beckoning for me because it seemed as though they were sort of in the middle of the street trying to get someone's attention. But somehow I felt that their beckoning was like waving me on actually, and saying, "Here we are, welcome, come."

As I walked slowly in their direction, they came running toward me. Sure enough, they were the three sons of Pastor Nouh. He had sent them out to see when I arrived based on the time I had said the bus would arrive, and to make sure that I was led to his home. Pastor Nouh's three sons were Jean, Daniel, and Israel.

When we met, they said, "Welcome, Uncle! Welcome, Uncle!" Of course I was happy to meet them. They led me to their home, and I met their father. We embraced each other for one or two minutes. It was a very heartfelt meeting. My heart was gripped by this compassionate man. We bonded instantly. That sense of bonding and unity reminds me of Psalm 133:1 (NKJV): "Behold, how good and how pleasant it is for brethren to dwell together in unity!" We sat down and talked for a while, and then we went across the street to a big restaurant and had lunch.

This was on a Saturday, and the rationale was that he wouldn't be in classes or studying; still, I did not want to take too much of his time. We were enjoying each other's fellowship so much after lunch that we talked late into the evening. Then it occurred to me that it might be possible to stay overnight and have fellowship with him the following day in his church.

He was happy to hear that I wanted to stay for fellowship. He said that it would not be a problem because he had a place for me to stay and he encouraged me to do just that. I had one little bag with me for the day. I ended up staying overnight, and we went to the church where he fellowshipped the following day.

During that time together, he told me a lot about his country, Mali, and Timbuktu, the city where he was a pastor. As Pastor Nouh told me about Timbuktu, my mind went back to the first time I heard the word *Timbuktu*. I was about four years old.

I used to go with my family to a park along the banks of the Ohio River to celebrate holidays or have parties in Cincinnati, where I was born and reared. My mom used to say to me that this particular park was as far as Timbuktu. Actually, it was only about 15 miles from the city, but that was a long way 75 years ago in terms of the transportation that was necessary for us to take to go there. Another instance when I heard the name of Timbuktu was when my mom would threaten to discipline me by "knocking me as far as Timbuktu." At those particular times I knew that Timbuktu was nowhere near, and of course, with her statement, I would correct my disobedient actions.

Before I left Brother Nouh's home, he did indicate that once he returned home, he was going to invite me to come and visit him. At the time I was thinking: *Is he kidding? Timbuktu is so far away and almost impossible to get to. It would take too much time and too much money to get there. Timbuktu is in the desert and I would have to ride a camel...* It seemed an entirely remote possibility that I would ever visit Pastor Nouh in Timbuktu, and all kinds of reasons and excuses not to go crossed my mind.

———•———

After I returned home from this first meeting in Philadelphia, Pastor Nouh and I stayed in touch during his time of studying, and my family and I also attended his graduation. We were happy to see his wife and sons on this glorious day when Pastor Nouh received his master's degree in community and economic development.

After we attended his graduation, he was scheduled to return to Timbuktu. Before he left the country however, his missionary sponsors expressed their desire to take him on a tour of New York City so he could see some destinations such as the World Trade Center, the United Nations, the Statue of Liberty, and Coney Island. When the sponsors saw that we were interested in dialoguing with him and his family, and spending as much time with them as we could before he went back to Timbuktu, they suggested that since we lived in New York, maybe we would like to take the family on the tour. My wife and I thought that was a really good idea. We could pick them up in Philadelphia, bring them back to New York to take the tours, and then take them to a sponsor's home in upstate New York where they were to live for some weeks before returning home to Timbuktu. My guess is that the sponsors did not insist on doing it themselves because of the time and expense involved. It was all good though. They would save money which could be used for the family in other ways and we were glad to do it; by this time our hearts were bound with Pastor Nouh's family.

It was an exciting few days. We picked up the family in Philadelphia, drove to our home in Queens, New York, and had wonderful fellowship as they stayed with us for a few days. We took them on lots of tours. We went to the United Nations, and while we were in the general assembly's main chamber where the nations of the world meet, I remember saying to Pastor Nouh, "In 10, 15, 20 years, your sons will be sitting on the platform representing Mali and the city of Timbuktu." It was just a passing thought, but Pastor Nouh said it was inspiring to him. After the United Nations, we went to Coney Island with its famed boardwalk, beach and amusement park. The boys went on the roller coasters; although the rides were terrifying, they seemed to enjoy it immensely. Our son Daniel, then about 16, and our daughter Lisa, then about 13, absolutely refused to ride the infamous Cyclone roller coaster.

One day we were discussing whether to visit the World Trade Center or the Statue of Liberty. There was not enough time to visit both. The lively discussion went back and forth, with the young people wanting to visit the Statue of Liberty and several of the adults, including Pastor Nouh, wanting to visit the World Trade Center. Pastor Nouh really pushed for the World Trade Center so we finally agreed to visit the "twin towers." This turned out to be a fortuitous choice because, of course, two years later on September 11, 2001, the World Trade Center was destroyed by terrorists. Years later Pastor Nouh mentioned that he was so glad he pushed for us to visit the twin towers; the opportunity would have been lost forever had we visited the Statue of Liberty. Fortunately, the Statue of Liberty still stands.

The view from the top of the World Trade Center was not only breathtaking, it was amazing to see New York City below, especially for Pastor Nouh and his family who were born and reared in the desert. They had never seen anything like that; we were up so high that the cars below looked like tiny bugs. The family was ecstatic for this never to be forgotten experience and we were delighted to be there with them. We said things about the greatness of God, about how awesome He is in giving people the intellect and skill to create such a marvel and also to create cities such as New York. In Psalm 8:3-6 (NKJV), the psalmist marvels at the greatness of God and the abilities He has given man:

> When I consider Your heavens, the work of Your fingers, The moon and the stars, which You have ordained, What is man that you are mindful of him, and the son of man that You visit him? For You have made him a little lower than the angels, And You have crowned him with glory and honor. You have made him to have dominion over the works of Your hands; You have put all things under his feet.

After visiting the World Trade Center, it was getting late, but we wanted to show Pastor Nouh and his family a few local places. We headed back toward our home in East Elmhurst, a neighborhood of Queens and stopped briefly in Flushing, also located in Queens, about 15 minutes from our home. We arrived at a historical site called the Bowne House, just before it closed. This site used to be the home of John Bowne, a Quaker who fought against slavery in the 1700s. The Quakers are a religious sect that is convinced that slavery is wrong and against God's purposes. They often broke unfair laws and risked going to jail or losing everything in order to help runaway slaves. The Quakers were active in Flushing. The Bowne House was a "stop" on the "Underground Railroad"—a system of safe houses used to shelter runaway slaves on their journey escaping to freedom. Near the Bowne House is a large shiny rock with the name of George Fox engraved on it. Fox was a Quaker preacher. Another indication of the activity of Quakers in the area is that the oldest Quaker meetinghouse in the U.S. is about one block away from the Bowne House and Fox's Rock. The Quaker meetinghouse was also a "stop" on the Underground Railroad. Flushing has a lot of history, some of which we were able to share with Brother Nouh and his family.

After spending time with us in our home for a few days, we drove the Nouh family to upstate New York where they were to stay with their missionary sponsors for several months until their return home. We met the sponsors and they shared with us how they came in contact with Pastor Nouh many years before when he was a young man. They mentioned that when they were missionaries in Timbuktu, they met him and had been exercised to sponsor him for years. They laughingly shared that as a young man Pastor Nouh and his friends came during siesta time and helped themselves to the vegetables in their garden without asking permission. After getting to know him, they were eventually able to entice him to attend Christian camp where he was saved.

After a few months, but before he left for his country, Pastor Nouh again strongly and lovingly encouraged me to prayerfully consider visiting Timbuktu. After much prayer, after discussing it with my wife, and after wrestling long and hard with the Lord, I finally had peace about going to Timbuktu. I began thinking of when and how I would make an effort to go to Timbuktu. I looked into the possibility and found out I could travel via Air France from Kennedy Airport in New York to Paris, France, and then take a connecting flight to Bamako, the capital of Mali.

I began to email Pastor Nouh about maybe coming to his country. He assured me that there was a family in Bamako who would receive me and allow me to come to their home and put me up for a day or two until I could make a connecting flight from Bamako to Timbuktu, about 700 miles north of Bamako in the desert.

Chapter Two

First Journey to Mali

In spite of what seemed overwhelming odds, the Lord allowed me to be received in Bamako by Pastor Nouh's friend whom I will call Brother S. M. He took me to his home which was a small compound or campus. There were college students on his compound living in small rooms. They went to various colleges in the area but had come to Brother S.M.'s to take advantage of a safe and godly environment, as well as the advice and encouragement of this powerful man of God.

I had a lovely room to myself. There was also a space on the compound where I could sit and observe the other activities going on around the compound, and be cared for and looked after in a personal way.

Once I arrived in Bamako, we made plans for me to fly to Timbuktu. There were four basic ways to get to Timbuktu from Bamako: one was to fly; one was by the *Niger Express,* a motorized boat traveling down the Niger River and which would take at least seven full days; a third way was by camel or donkey, and the fourth way was to drive a vehicle. The roads were not modern; motorists needed a jeep or some type of four-wheel drive that could navigate the bad roads and be able to get out if stuck in the sand. For me, flying was definitely the best option, especially in view of the short time I had to visit Timbuktu. There was a small, Russian airline usually flying to Timbuktu Mondays, Wednesdays and Fridays, so I planned to leave on a Monday after attending church service with the family in Bamako. This enabled me to spend a little over a full week in Timbuktu. Altogether, I was in Mali for three weeks. This was my first trip to Timbuktu; the year was 2000.

After arriving in Bamako, I called Brother Nouh. Fortunately, he had a telephone. I let him know I arrived safely and we were able to plan for my arrival in Timbuktu. The day came for leaving Bamako; it took about three hours to fly to Timbuktu, with one stop at Mopti, a northern city between Bamako and Timbuktu. I arrived around four o'clock in Timbuktu.

———•———

Brother Nouh was ecstatic to see me. With much excitement, he met me at the airport, took me to his home, and made me feel very comfortable. The following morning, after breakfast, Brother Nouh took me to the roof of his home. Brother Nouh's home is not very elaborate. It is made partly of mud bricks and partly of limestone. In the desert, because of the intense heat, people have homes like his, with a flat roof so that during the summer months at nighttime they can sleep on the roof because it's cooler than inside the home.

As we walked on the roof that morning, Pastor Nouh pointed to an area surrounding the city which he called "the Belt of Misery." This human ring of nomadic people surrounds Timbuktu; people come in from the vast Sahara. When there's little rain in the desert, water sources dry up and there are no green shrubs for the camels, sheep, goats, and donkeys; nor is there food and water for the people. Out of desperation, thousands of people move toward the city of Timbuktu. They try to get water, food, clothing, and any possible handouts in order to sustain themselves. Pastor Nouh estimated that depending on the season and the water levels, as many as 40-50,000 people make up the Belt of Misery. As the people in the Belt of Misery surround the city, they pitch their tents. This is where they cook, eat, sleep, and carry on the necessary activities for survival.

When Brother Nouh showed me the Belt of Misery on my first visit to Timbuktu, the Lord gave me a tremendous burden for these unreached people. Those suffering in the Belt of Misery are only a small number of the unreached millions in the Sahara who often die from a lack of water, food, and health care. In later years after visiting Timbuktu two more times, I became very active in burdening my fellow believers for the country of Mali, especially for the city of Timbuktu. God has placed a special burden on my heart for the people in this region of the world. The Lord burdened me to gather clothing, shoes, reading glasses, and other miscellaneous items and send them for distribution to various cities in the region through Pastor Nouh's church in Timbuktu.

———•———

One of the blessings I experienced each Saturday morning during my first visit to Timbuktu was accompanying Brother Nouh to a particular building in Timbuktu where there was a radio transformer that beamed the Gospel throughout the desert. This was unheard of in many Muslim states; no infidel, that is, no Christian, would be allowed to get on the radio and speak to Muslims about Christianity in a Muslim state. I experienced it as a work of the Holy Spirit.

It is crucial that God's Word go forth, and He has promised that it will be effective in getting into the hearts and minds of those who hear it: "So is my word that goes out from my mouth: It will not return to me empty, but will accomplish what I desire and achieve the purpose for which I sent it" (Isaiah 55:11, NIV).

Each Saturday Pastor Nouh would go and speak through the radio transformer, and many of the people who had transistor radios with batteries could listen to the Gospel as well as stay in contact with the outside world. Pastor Nouh told me an amazing story about the radio ministry which demonstrates the truth not only of Isaiah 55:11, but also of Hebrews 4:12 (NIV):

"For the word of God is living and active. Sharper than any double-edged sword, it penetrates even to dividing soul and spirit, joints and marrow; it judges the thoughts and attitudes of the heart."

The amazing story regarding the radio ministry was this: in March 1999, a Malian military officer led six Tuaregs of the Kel Antassar tribe who lived northwest of Timbuktu in the Sahara to Pastor Nouh at the church with a message. "Our great *marabout* (West African Muslim priest) has sent us before you to have you explain and help us to understand the vision of an apparition of Jesus which we have seen in the desert."

Pastor Nouh asked them to describe what they saw. Some of them said, "He was riding a horse and was holding a sword." According to the *Hadiths* (Islamic traditions), the only prophet and messenger of Allah who will come back holding a sword is Jesus. This is why they kept saying it was Jesus.

Others in this group said, "No, He was flying at two meters above the ground, holding a book in which was written the name of Jesus."

Pastor Nouh was determined that these men would not go away without hearing about God's salvation plan through Jesus. He went from Genesis to Revelation and explained about the fall and the redemption of all of humanity by Jesus Christ.

Pastor Nouh told them that what they had seen must be an apparition of the Antichrist because the *Injil Issa* (New Testament) explains clearly that Jesus warned people not to search for Him in the desert or in inner rooms: "Therefore if they say to you, 'Look, He is in the desert!' do not go out; or 'Look, He is in the inner rooms!' do not believe it. For as the lightning comes from the east and flashes to the west, so also will the coming of the Son of Man be" (Matthew 24:26-27, NKJV). Of course, the apparition could have been God's way of leading them to someone who could share the truth with them. In either case, Pastor Nouh warned them all to read and take seriously the Gospel of Jesus Christ because everything He has said will happen exactly as predicted.

The good news is that these men from the Muslim priest took the Gospel back to their people in the desert. One fortunate result of this incident is that the men who were sent by their Muslim priest repeated the story to many in the city of Timbuktu, and soon announcers on FM radio stations in the area were all talking about the return of Jesus. This opened up a number of opportunities to the church for evangelism and led to a number of presentations about Jesus in nomadic camps, massive distributions of Christian literature in the cities in the region, as well as the sending of missionaries from national denominations. Eventually, some Christian groups were able to get access to their own FM radio programs, daily broadcasting the Gospel of Jesus Christ for hours. Also, the evangelism team from Pastor Nouh's church did follow up in their communities. One of the Tuareg men who came to Christ entered a Bible institute for pastoral studies. I was blessed to hear what God was doing.

———•———

Pastor Nouh shared this story with me the same morning that he explained about Timbuktu's Belt of Misery. Of course, many of the people who came in from the desert had heard about the Evangelical Baptist Church that Pastor Nouh leads. Many of them would make their way over to the church just to see if there might be handouts of any kind or anything to help them. They knew that the message of the Gospel is one of love and concern in terms of helping people; they heard from others that not only did the Christians at the church share the Gospel message, they also showed love and concern in practical ways. A water well was built by the church and operated electrically from the church itself. Needless to say, water in the midst of a desert is a source of life. You can imagine the number of people from the Belt of Misery who came to the church to get fresh water from the well. Believers from the church always issued a warm, loving invitation to visit the church on Sunday. For those who did attend a church service, communication was not a problem since the message was sometimes translated into as many as five languages.

Pastor Nouh's church, the Evangelical Baptist Church came about in an unusual way. Since

Timbuktu is a Muslim city, not only did Pastor Nouh have to ask for permission from the authorities to erect a church building, the site also had to be approved. When Pastor Nouh humbly went to the officials to ask permission, at first they refused. Later they told him that the only location they could think of was a place where it was known that demons lived and hung out. The officials warned Pastor Nouh that he and his people would be eaten alive. Pastor Nouh and the church members accepted the location. Actually, the church members built a beautiful building and thrived. Far from being eaten alive, the demons were driven out by the Holy Spirit.

Once he was a little concerned because one of the tribal leaders from the desert wanted to meet and talk with him. Pastor Nouh felt this leader had questions about his motives, and he was a little apprehensive since it appeared that the leader was coming to discuss what he had heard over the radio. So Pastor Nouh took precautions. He had family members around him when this man came.

As it turned out, there was nothing to fear. Pastor Nouh and the others stood amazed as this tribal leader shared that so many of his people had come to him in the desert about dreams and visions they had been having after listening to the radio broadcasts. The dreams and visions were about the Lord Jesus Christ, but they had never heard the story before. They wanted to know the meaning of it all. So this leader was coming to Pastor Nouh to ask some questions about the Gospel message. The people told the leader that they had several visions of a man dressed in white, confirming Pastor's Nouh's words about the Gospel. Fortunately, Pastor Nouh spoke the language of this leader and explained to him very clearly the Gospel of Jesus Christ from a humble, broken posture. This man took the Gospel of Jesus Christ back to his people in the Sahara.

———•———

On the Tuesday evening after I arrived, the church had the women's Bible class, and Brother Nouh encouraged me to attend. He also asked if I wanted to speak. This gave me pause because before going to Timbuktu, I asked the Lord to give me a humble, broken spirit. I did not want to go to Timbuktu as a Westerner—as an American having all the answers who could solve all the problems of the masses in the desert. I asked the Lord to help me to learn from this man of God, learn from his people, observe and dialogue with them and communicate the best I could through a translator. I said this to Brother Nouh, and he was a little surprised. He thought that coming from the West, I would have something special to say, or would take the posture of a missionary. I believe the Lord helped me try not to do that. So Brother Nouh conducted the Bible class.

During the early years of my life, at Bible school and missionary conferences, and in talking with missionaries in general, somehow I'd gotten the picture from the posture of much of Western Christianity that no one else had the answers. It seemed that the way visitors to Asia, Africa and South America presented Jesus Christ was so authoritative, it came across very strong to many of us African Americans even in America. When white people came to our community, the attitude was, "We came here not because we had to; we came here because we wanted to, and we've come to help you, so we expect you to fall in line and submit to whatever we tell you." I am sure that missionaries and others really didn't mean it this way and sometimes I may have been misreading their attitude. But that's how many of us African Americans here in America experienced other groups coming into our community: talking down to us, and speaking in a way that encouraged us to recognize them as a grand source of authority. One story that was shared with me indicated how some of the missionaries treated the local people. A missionary who had been in Timbuktu for many years hired this particular lady to work at his compound. It gripped my heart when I heard that even though there were two or three cars on the compound, this Malian lady had to walk to and from the compound for 14 years. Never once was she graciously picked up in the morning or dropped off at her home in the evening.

It was a 12-mile round trip! I was saddened when I heard this because the missionary's behavior did not demonstrate the love of God. After traveling in several countries and meeting missionaries and visiting them on their compounds, I noticed other signs of this kind of hierarchy. Some of them live in enclosures behind walls that keep some of the local people out. Also, their cars and other conveniences make it clear that they had resources from the U.S. They had a standard of living that was quite different from the local people.

As I moved among people in different countries during my travels, I found out that many of the local people didn't trust the missionaries and would not open up to them. I saw this as a tremendous hindrance to our American brothers and sisters presenting the Gospel to native inhabitants. I very much wanted to avoid coming across as though I thought I was superior and knew everything.

In addition to the women's Tuesday night Bible study in Timbuktu, there was a Bible class for the fellowship in general on Thursdays at the Evangelical Baptist Church under the leadership of Brother Nouh. And of course, Sunday was the formal time for worship. Believers came from all over Timbuktu for the time of worship and hearing the Word of God. There was also Sunday school on Sunday mornings, and one of the beautiful things I experienced was that Brother Nouh's son Daniel taught a Sunday school class with students ages nine to about 14. The amazing thing about these students is that they memorized whole chapters of the Bible. It was quite different from here in America, where there are many publishers, such as Urban Ministries, David C. Cook, Standard, and denominational groups and others producing Sunday school materials. These students in Timbuktu did not have any study aids other than the Bible and they committed large portions of the Bible to memory. I was quite impressed: this was a tremendous testimony to their love for the Word of God and their commitment to hide God's Word in their heart. And of course, that's the way it was done in the early church.

These were some of the things I was learning and seeing, to say nothing about when Brother Nouh would get up and speak and share the Word of God. His ministry of the Word was a real blessing. There would be preaching in French, the official language, and an interpreter to translate, if necessary, into various languages, including Arabic, Sonrai, Ashanti, Bambara, Tamasheq, Soninke, Dogon, or English; the goal is to make sure that all attending could understand the message. The church is a multicultural experience, and by God's grace there I was sitting and learning, and being mesmerized by the functioning of this church as the Word of God was going out in a Muslim country. I felt highly privileged and fortunate as I realized that by God's grace I was one of the few foreign individuals allowed to experience that.

There is one other Protestant church in the city, the Assembly of God Church of Timbuktu, led by Pastor

Nouh's brother-in-law, Pastor Bouya. This pastor was led to Christ and discipled by Pastor Nouh; at one time he was Nouh's assistant pastor. I had the opportunity to visit and speak there as well as at Pastor Nouh's church. I was impressed by the fact that the Assembly of God Church had developed a large farm in the desert. This was set up to help people be economically self-sustaining. The large plot of land was divided into smaller lots; individuals could rent a lot and grow vegetables. The Assembly of God denomination had raised more than 25 million dollars to develop their ministry under Pastor Bouya's leadership. They had a vision for a Bible school and a huge church building. I saw the partially finished building that was to become a Bible school; construction had temporarily stopped. I also saw the plot of land for the projected church building which was about half the size of a football field. The pastor and his home and church featured more of the Western style than a Malian culture-in-the-desert model.

—•—

On Sunday evenings, many believers came to Brother Nouh's home for a time of fellowship. A few more came because they knew this foreigner Hoise Birks was there and they wanted to look at him and pick up any other bits of information they could get. They came, and I was humbled to feel that level of interest and concern and love, as many of them would smile at me and ask Pastor Nouh to translate certain statements, greetings, and prayer requests; they assured me that they would pray for me, my family, and my ministry.

Often in the evenings after Brother Nouh would return home and after supper, he would allow me to have extended times of conversation with him, to ask various questions and hear his responses. Quite often I was just astounded at the history he shared with me about Timbuktu, the church, his own testimony, his family, some of the aspirations of his own heart, and some of the threats upon the church. Our talks went on through the night, sometimes until about 11 or 12 o'clock at night. By habit Pastor Nouh gets up every morning at four. I felt a little guilty at times and tried to back off, but he encouraged me to take the time while I had it, assuring me that he would let me know when it was over and we had to go to bed.

One of the things he shared with me was about Kirsamba, a village 30 miles southwest of Timbuktu consisting of a whole community of black Jews. The history of these people goes all the way back to Morocco and Egypt. In that part of the world, Egypt is really within walking distance. And of course, in a Muslim state, we can understand why Jews were corralled or gathered into one little village, as Muslims are not very friendly to Jews at all, even though they were black Jews. I often think of the boldness of Brother Nouh to not only give his sons biblical names, but to name his youngest son Israel. This is an astounding thing to do in a Muslim community. It took boldness and courage and is a powerful testimony of his faith.

Chapter Three

A Liberation Machine and Ancient Knowledge

Often in the morning as I walked through the streets of Timbuktu, I saw two or three women using a pestle to pound grains in a hewed-out bowl. Women would put grains inside the mortar and pound them, crushing the seeds.

One morning I watched two ladies pound grain at least 150 times with the club-like pestle. I counted them. That is a lot of work, and it would be for only one meal, breakfast. The women had to repeat the same process for the noon and supper meals. When you multiply two ladies pounding 150 strokes each, that's 300 strokes. At noontime that comes to 600, and at supper that comes to 900. So I was almost sweating just looking at these ladies work like that to prepare a simple meal.

Muslims had centers where people could bring their grains and have them crushed and divided by a machine. But they would not allow the Christians to bring their grains to these centers. That's often the case in a Muslim state. Christians do not have access to some of the conveniences that Muslims have, and they make it clear: Don't come to us, don't expect us to help you; the fact of the matter is we're trying to get rid of you. So the Christians wouldn't go anywhere near.

The Lord spoke to my heart upon arriving back in America to burden my home church and other Christians to prayerfully consider buying such a machine that could be purchased in Mali so that the church in Timbuktu might have one for themselves, and perhaps charge a small fee to other people who came to them to have their grains processed by this machine.

As I thought of the drudgery involved in pounding grain, and as I prayed while back home about doing something to help, my wife and I began calling the grain processing machine the "liberation machine" because it would liberate women from the arduous task of pounding grain daily to feed their families. I reasoned, and the women confirmed this, that if the Christian women in Timbuktu could have such a machine, it would not only liberate them from drudgery, it would free up time for them to do God's work.

When I came back to the United States I had tears in my eyes as I shared with local churches the need for a "liberation machine" to help the believers in Timbuktu. Not only did I emphasize the drudgery, I shared with them that such a machine could free up these Christian women for more evangelism and more talking and sharing with Muslim women the Gospel of Jesus Christ. Within a few months, there was a generous response from the believers in the United States, and more than $6,000 was given toward a liberation machine. I was able to put this money in the hands of Brother Nouh and he purchased the machine in Bamako, Mali. He had it loaded on a truck, and he rode with it in the truck all the way to Timbuktu. On a subsequent trip to Timbuktu, I was really encouraged to see how very helpful the liberation machine has proven to be. One evening, a group of women from the church had a special ceremony of African praise dance at the liberation machine. It was wonderful to see. I assured those who contributed to this machine that it is a great blessing, especially to the women who used to have to spend hours pounding grain with a mortar and pestle.

Now that the liberation machine is in place, these Christian Malian women are more available to witness to other Muslim women. It is almost impossible for a man to witness to a Muslim woman; she is forbidden to speak to men outside of her family members, and in some Muslim countries women are not allowed to venture out without being accompanied by a male relative. I often say that when Muslim women are taught to read and write, and are liberated by the

Gospel of Jesus Christ, there will be a revolution among Muslims such as the world has never seen.

Speaking of literacy, in 2005, the believers who speak Tamasheq celebrated the completion of the New Testament in their Tamasheq language. It took 13 years and Pastor Nouh helped with the translation project. Although the official language of Mali is French, only 20 percent of the people are literate. Many of the ordinary people are not fluent in French; 36 languages and dialects are spoken. It is impossible to overestimate the value of having the Bible in their own language.

———•———

In addition to the liberation machine, another ministry I began after visiting Timbuktu the first time was the reading glasses ministry. On my first visit to Timbuktu, I felt led to take several dozen reading glasses and distribute them. On my second trip, Pastor Nouh's son Jean and I were passing by a home and a lady was trying to get our attention. She was smiling and talking excitedly, so I asked Jean what she was saying. He said that she was thanking me for the reading glasses. Evidently the reading glasses had opened up a whole new world for her, and for others who had received them. Many had poor eyesight after years of damage from the wind, sun, and the sand. Their eyes suffer greatly from the relentless bright sun and the dust storms as they bear the discomfort of living at the "door to the Sahara."

Once I realized how helpful the reading glasses were, I committed to a ministry of sending dozens and dozens of reading glasses to Timbuktu over a period of at least ten years. I found a place in New York City where I bought the glasses very cheaply and mailed them to Timbuktu.

Pastor Nouh told me that the reading glasses have taken him to places that he otherwise would have been unable to go. Also, as a result of distributing the reading glasses, he received visitors who would otherwise never visit him. From time to time, Pastor Nouh and his wife Fati have the opportunity to share their testimonies or give out some Christian literature along with the reading glasses. Since God promises that His word does not come back to Him empty, but accomplishes what He pleases (Isaiah 55:11), only eternity will reveal the fruit of the reading glasses ministry.

——●——

Brother Nouh is a brilliant, intellectual scholar of literature, history and culture; he knows the Muslim scholars in Timbuktu and all of them highly respect him. He pointed out one or two of them to me during walks we took. They would look at him and greet him affectionately at a distance, and that itself is saying a lot in a Muslim culture; usually when people know who

Christians are, they make it a point to avoid them. In contrast, their leading scholars showed respect to this "infidel," thereby acknowledging the good that this compassionate man of God was doing in their community. Also, he is active in the civic affairs of the city, and while I was there, an important government official came to his home to invite him to an event honoring a visiting French official (Mali is a former French colony). It is unusual for a Muslim official to enter the home of an "infidel," but this official did so because God has given Pastor Nouh favor in the eyes of the Muslim officials.

On two different occasions, we attended meetings of city business, and Pastor Nouh and I were seated on the platform with civic and religious leaders. On one occasion, we were seated in places of honor with five leading Muslim priests, or imams. Each greeted Pastor Nouh warmly. He told me later that each of them had gratefully received a pair of reading glasses. For many years Pastor Nouh has been involved in human rights work and in peacemaking efforts. He participates in most of the conferences and meetings calling for reconciliation and peace in northern Mali. In December 2011 he participated in a conference called the Program for Peace and Development in the northern Mali town of Ségou. In February 2012 he was among seven participants who represented the Timbuktu Region at the National Forum on Peace and Security in a city called Kayes. Like Joseph and

Daniel in the Bible, Pastor Nouh is often sought out for his wisdom and advice.

———•———

So it was in due time that Brother Nouh introduced me to the Honorable Dr. Haidara. Dr. Haidara is a Muslim scholar and a brilliant intellectual who is at the forefront of preserving one of Mali's richest treasures, ancient manuscripts. These manuscripts document the learning and wisdom of the country's glory days. Dr. Haidara gathered many ancient manuscripts from private homes in Timbuktu and the surrounding desert; his family also owned many manuscripts.

In Timbuktu, there are manuscripts passed down from generation to generation for hundreds of years; families would store the manuscripts away, often in metal trunks to preserve them from the ravages of the desert. Unfortunately, sometimes the manuscript would be destroyed by ants or termites. Sometimes the paper would break down and become brittle after being exposed for so long to the intense arid heat. It is common in Timbuktu for families to have ancient manuscripts stored away. They are highly cherished and considered a family legacy, so much so that the Malian government eventually placed a ban on taking them out of the country.

It is a race to preserve this precious legacy before it crumbles and blows away. Others have recognized the need to protect the manuscripts and the Malian government has obtained funding from Kuwait, the U.S., Norway, South Africa, Luxemburg, and from the Science and Culture arm of the United Nations. Dr. Haidara was able to gather many of these manuscripts, including those of his family, and later he opened a museum displaying the manuscripts.

———•———

By God's grace, I had the opportunity to be invited to his home. I saw firsthand thousands of manuscripts in metal suitcases in his home. This came about when one day Brother Nouh encouraged his son Jean to take me to the home of Dr. Haidara. Brother Nouh and Dr. Haidara are close friends and have a strong relationship even though he is Muslim and Brother Nouh is Christian. When we arrived at Dr. Haidara's home, he served Jean and me hot tea as we sat on the floor. He talked about the historical value of the manuscripts and the importance of keeping them in Mali. He shared with me that many nations, including France and the U.S. were interested in these manuscripts, and would do almost anything to get possession of them. Some foreigners even wanted to market the manuscripts and make millions on them. But of course, this wasn't possible. In spite of the nations, universities, societies, and museums that wanted the manuscripts, Dr. Haidara is in full control of the manuscripts in his possession and he is committed to making sure the rich legacy of Mali's scholarship remains in Mali. As

I looked at the thousands of manuscripts in his home in metal trunks in a storage room, I was just amazed, speechless actually.

As I looked at the manuscripts, I felt humbled to be in the presence of such a legacy. I was an African American in the ancient city of Timbuktu, where scholars would come from all parts of the world to study at the famed Sankore University. This university grew out of the Sankore mosque and much of the learning in the universities in Egypt came from this university. Many say that the famous Greek philosophers got their information from Egyptian philosophy, and the Egyptian philosophers, in turn, got their information from African institutions like the University of Sankore in Mali during the Golden Age of Timbuktu in the 15th and 16th centuries. Scholars would not only study Islam, but also medicine, mathematics, chemistry, physics, and astronomy, to name a few subjects.

Some of the manuscripts in Timbuktu are over 600 years old and include poetry by women, legal reflections, as well as innovative scientific treatises. These manuscripts have reshaped ideas about African and Islamic civilizations. Contrary to the popular beliefs of many Europeans that Africa has no history, only darkness, these manuscripts prove that black Africa was a haven of high literacy with a rich intellectual heritage when the Renaissance was barely stirring in Europe.

Here I was, in the presence of manuscripts containing all of this learning. So much of this knowledge is preserved in the manuscripts. I was grateful to be experiencing this firsthand.

———•———

Pastor Nouh is like a walking encyclopedia. He has carefully studied his country's history and culture and he is able to rattle off facts and dates with ease. Of course, all of the many tours he gives visitors keep his mind sharp.

Pastor Nouh gave me information about the origin of the Sankore Mosque. It is an unusual story. According to Pastor Nouh, it is said that a very fair skinned or white lady paid to have the Sankore Mosque built. No one knows her name, but she was said to be from a tribe called the Laglal. When she built the mosque, there was no Muslim priest for the mosque. When she was asked why build a mosque without a priest, she predicted that after her death a white Lord (Sankore means "white Lord" in the Sonrai language) would come and be the first priest of the mosque. Forty years after her death, a white Lord named Agqib came from the desert. No one knows what his identity was or where he came from, or which tribe or family he was from. He came and took the keys and became the first priest of the mosque. He changed the shape of the mosque and gave the sanctuary the same cuboid shape as the Kaaba in Mecca. More importantly, there was an annex connected to the mosque which was first used as a huge Koranic school and eventually became Sankore University.

Centuries ago, thousands of students and hundreds of scholars came from all over Africa, the Middle East, Europe, and Turkey and convened and studied or taught at the university. It is said that it took scholars about ten years to complete the highest level of their course work, the equivalent of a doctorate in the West. The 15th and 16th centuries were the Golden Age of the university with more than 100,000 people in Timbuktu and more than 25,000 students attending Sankore University. (When I was there for my third visit in 2006, the population of Timbuktu was about 50,000.)

Because of the prestige and influence of Sankore University, books and manuscripts were the most exchanged products of ancient times. Emperors of the Songhai Empire played a significant role in funding the scholars to teach and to copy the vast store of knowledge at that time. Even today, according to Pastor Nouh, there are manuscripts from Timbuktu at Oxford and Cambridge in England, the Sorbonne in France, and Harvard in the United States. The Ford Foundation has a special partnership with the owners of ancient manuscripts in Timbuktu. Many have already been translated from Arabic into English and French. An example of this is the translation of the

famous historical chronologies of West Africa called
the *Tarikh al-Fattash* and the *Tarikh al-Sudan.*

Chapter Four

The Value of Guides

While the Sankore Mosque represents much that is ancient in Timbuktu, the water tower represents much that is modern. Once as Jean, Pastor Nouh's son, and I were exploring the city, we passed a water tower that had been constructed by the government. It's a modern water tower, and not the original water well around which Timbuktu was developed. It was breathtaking to see such a structure in Timbuktu. I had the opportunity to take a picture of this water well, an amazing structure, and it's included in this book so many will see it for the first time.

As is true in any desert area, water is crucial. Pastor Nouh is a consultant concerning water resources and conservation for the city and the surrounding areas. He was asked by city officials to assist in finding areas where possibly large quantities of water could be found and taken from the ground. He has helped, with the support of Westerners, dozens of villages and camps in the surrounding areas to get their own drilled and cone wells.

Once he took me and his three sons to an area near the Niger River, which flows approximately eight miles from Timbuktu. A wealthy man wanted to plant a grove of eucalyptus trees and he asked Pastor Nouh if he could find an area in the desert that would be suitable. We met the man at a prearranged site and Pastor Nouh suggested an area to plant the trees where they would have natural irrigation.

Of course I could not be in Timbuktu without experiencing a camel ride. Brother Nouh ordered a short, brief camel ride into one of the nearby suburbs of Timbuktu. Tourists that come to Timbuktu are often encouraged to take a camel ride to a suburb to experience nomadic life; it is a way to allow tourists to experience the history and culture of the people. When the camel came and knelt down, I looked at the camel and the camel looked at me. I was about 250 pounds then, but they were encouraging me to get on the camel. It was quite a process. As you get on the camel, you sit in a saddle behind the hump toward the back of the camel and you rest your feet at the base of the camel's neck. The driver of the camel says some words and the camel gets up from its kneeling position. In my case, the camel leaned forward with his hind legs and I almost fell on my face. He then brought his two front feet up under him, and by then I was ready to get down and run. But I remember Sister Fati, Pastor Nouh's wife, encouraging me: "Don't leave, stay, ride the camel."

Even though I was frightened, I stayed on and we went to a small suburb of Timbuktu. As part of that experience, the local people spread a mat and serve the tourist a cup of hot tea in the desert. Everyone talks and visits for a while, and then the tourist gets back on the camel and comes back to the city of Timbuktu proper. By the time I got to the village, my stomach was upset and churning because of the waddling and the bouncing of the camel. Everything I had on my stomach from the noon meal came up. The people were used to such experiences, and all they did was cover the food that came out of my belly with sand. Had they not done this, within seconds, certainly minutes, there would have been thousands of flies all around the place and they were not about to allow that to happen.

As I sat on the ground, a young Arab man who spoke English came near to me. He began to ask me questions, and I began to ask him questions. I complimented him on his excellent English. This young Arab man was obviously extremely intelligent. He began to share with me the potential of his country. He mentioned that oil was under the sand in Timbuktu and that the West was interested in his county because of its oil. He said that there are places in the desert where the oil can be seen coming through the ground. You can imagine I was speechless as he shared that pertinent information during my little excursion into the desert on the camel ride. After we had the tea, they rolled up the mats and we were on our way back to Timbuktu. I was following in the footsteps of many tourists.

Pastor Nouh is the head tourist guide official, appointed by the mayor of Timbuktu and by the National Minister of Tourism in Mali. He's extremely knowledgeable about the history, culture and peoples of Mali; his knowledge is not limited to the ways of the camel and the donkey.

In Timbuktu, there are basically four types of homes that people live in. The Arabs usually live in a structured, multileveled (usually two levels with a flat roof) white concrete building, like a condominium; this building indicates the highest social status. The next class lives in homes not quite as structured, built using mud for the interior and limestone bricks on the exterior. It is nice, but noticeably second class. The third class type of residential structure in Timbuktu is a three-room house of mud with a Turkish toilet; its wall provides some privacy to the family. The home of the poorer nomadic person is simply a hut made with supple tree limbs and overlaid with woven mats. It can be taken down, rolled up, and put on the back of a donkey or camel in an hour; it is ready to go almost immediately. When one sees these structures, the economic status of the dwellers is apparent.

———•———

Before I knew it, it was time to prepare to return to the United States. I'd experienced the lecture on the Belt of Misery, gone to the women's Tuesday night Bible classes and the church's Bible classes on Thursday, and experienced worship with the believers in Timbuktu under the ministry of Brother Nouh on Sunday.

During my time in Timbuktu, most days I was invited out each evening to a believer's home for supper. It was wonderful to get to know the people as they went out of their way to show me hospitality by inviting me into their homes and preparing a meal for me; for some, it was a stretch economically because they were so poor. Their custom was to sit on the floor and spread the food before them, but some felt uncomfortable having me sit on the floor and they wanted to put up a table for me. I assured them that I felt completely comfortable relaxing on the floor and eating with them. I wanted to eat the same way that the people ate. Some would say, "No, no, we've got to put up a table for you" and it took some convincing to get them to allow me to sit on the floor with them. After they saw how comfortable I was, they relented. It was beautiful to dialogue and relate to the people like that. Everything was arranged on the floor and in order, and it was just beautiful.

Pastor Nouh showed wisdom by arranging for me to visit different houses and get to know certain families. In this way, I could be open to hear about the fears, concerns, and burdens on their hearts. The believers had many questions, and we spent many hours sharing meals and discussing the Word of God. Both the believers and I were greatly encouraged.

My first trip to Timbuktu was a fantastic learning experience. I knew I would never forget the people, the sights, the sounds, the history, and the whirling sands of the desert. After backtracking to Bamako, France and arriving home in America, I chalked up my visit to Timbuktu as a historical experience, never to be repeated. Within months, however, my heart was drawn back to Timbuktu and I began to think in terms of visiting Timbuktu a second time. More than that, Pastor Nouh was lovingly encouraging me to prayerfully consider coming back. My heart was not finished with the ancient city. I knew there was much more to learn—no way could my three weeks in Mali even begin to scratch the surface of the additional rich learning experiences awaiting me.

As I prayed about it, my interest in returning grew, and after talking it over with my wife and praying about it with her, I had peace about visiting Timbuktu a second time in 2002.

Chapter Five

Rediscovery—Drawn Back to Timbuktu

One thing drawing me back to Timbuktu in 2002 was Pastor Nouh himself. He is such a courageous, godly, intelligent, and knowledgeable man and I highly respect him. I simply wanted to learn at his feet.

I was not the only one who respected Pastor Nouh. He is well thought of by the elders and officials in Timbuktu even though he is a Christian, a so-called infidel. Just the fact that he is allowed to run numerous Christian ministries in a hostile Islamic state is a testimony to the respect accorded him. The respect shown to Brother Nouh in Timbuktu was manifest in other ways. The city gives respect to him by giving him the key to the graveyard. Only three people had keys to the graveyard: the Catholic priest, the head Muslim priest, and Pastor Nouh.

One day during my second visit Pastor Nouh took me to see the graveyard. There were Christian graves amongst the Muslim graves, but the Christian graves were the only ones desecrated. The Muslims had broken down their crosses, and had taken a sledgehammer and tried to literally tear the gravestones down. More than likely they were not happy with Pastor Nouh for showing me the graveyard, even though he was acting in his official capacity as a tourist guide. Not only was he named Mali's foremost national tourist guide, he was honored in the city of Sikasso in 2004 as the first national guide for tourism in all of Mali; at this special occasion he won a "Prime" cane with the honor.

Another stop on a day tour, in addition to the graveyard, was a visit to the Grand Mosque of Timbuktu. As tour guide, Pastor Nouh would explain to tourists such as me the history of the mosque. This mosque was built by a king named Mansa Kanga Moussa in 1325-1327 A.D. This person left his city of Niani, which was near the capital Bamako, and went to Mecca. The round trip took one year. While in Mecca, he did something which made him famous. Mansa Moussa bought a portion of land for Malians who make a pilgrimage to Mecca and that land is still designated at present for the Malians who make the holy pilgrimage to Mecca.

When King Moussa returned to Mali, he brought a Spanish architect with him and he paid the architect 40 kilos of gold to build the Grand Mosque. Some say that he was the wealthiest person ever to have lived. For taking so much gold from his Malian kingdom to Mecca and for distributing so much gold on his pilgrimage, the price of gold fell for many years in the

Arab world. The mosque built by Mansa Moussa is called the Djinguereber Mosque, or the Great Mosque. Djinguereber means "great prayer" in the Sonrai language. The mosque is huge and is made entirely of mud. In 1985, it was classified by the United Nations Science and Culture division as a World Heritage Site. This huge mosque is still in use. People come to pray five times a day as required by Islamic law. The mosque is an important part of life in an Islamic state; in it the people receive religious teaching, and the imam (high priest) leads the prayers and provides religious guidance and counseling. It also provides the community's social connections.

Pastor Nouh took tourists on the roof of the mosque so that they could see a spectacular view of Timbuktu and the surrounding sand dunes of the Sahara; the reflection from these sand dunes looks like a kind of golden belt around the city. During the tour, he pointed out a place in the mosque where Muslims worshiped in front of a mausoleum honoring a figurative type of beast demon; this shows that there were high levels of occultism and superstition mixed in with the practice of Islam. Evidently this is not unusual in many countries where Islam is practiced in sub-Saharan Africa; it is classified as folk Islam.

———•———

Another destination for tourists is the Buktu Museum. In this museum are pictures and models of what the city was like as it was developing around an ancient water well. In one such picture, a woman named Buktu directed traffic. Somewhere between 1020 and 1050 AD, Buktu, a black slave woman was ordered by nomadic Tuaregs to regulate caravans when they came for water at the well. When the water level became low, Buktu sat by the well and regulated who should and who should not get water; she had to have unusual managerial skills to manage 20-30,000 nomadic families and their camels and livestock as they made their way to the well from the desert. They navigated by way of the stars.

The prefix "tin" is from the Tamasheq language and it means "belonging to," "place of," or the "the way to." Buktu means "the belly woman", so Timbuktu literally means "the place of the belly woman" or "belonging to the belly woman" or "the way to the belly woman." The city developed around this water well.

———•———

From its humble beginnings, Timbuktu grew from a seasonal settlement and became a permanent settlement early in the 12th century. Benefiting from a shift in trading routes, Timbuktu flourished from the trade in salt, gold, ivory, ostrich eggs and feathers, beads, fabric, animals for the circus, camels, horses, gunpowder, palm oil, sugar, syrup, wine, cola nuts, granite stones, and slaves. Some slaves were stolen, and some were taken captive in war and sold by their captors.

Pastor Nouh said that slaves went in three directions from Timbuktu. First, they went to Dakar, Senegal and on to the Caribbean. Second, they went to Tangier and Casablanca, Morocco, and on to Europe. Third, they crossed the Sahara (two-thirds died crossing the desert), arrived in Cairo and were sold to Arabs in the Middle East. According to Pastor Nouh, Arabs have taken three times as many slaves from Africa as Westerners, and at present Arabs are still taking slaves from Africa (under the modern practice of human trafficking). Not only did many of the slaves taken by the Arabs die while crossing the vast and hazardous Sahara, many were castrated for the purpose of serving in harems or for use as human shields for Arab troops. Slaves taken by Westerners, by contrast, were needed to work cotton and sugar plantations and were more valuable alive than dead; rather than castration, some male slaves were used as "studs" to impregnate women in order to increase the slave population.

In addition to a lucrative slave trade, some products were so plentiful during Timbuktu's Golden Age that a sultan was said to have exclaimed, "I am wondering if the sand dunes of Timbuktu are made of gold." Of course this was not true; Timbuktu was just a huge market for products to be sold and exchanged and had an auspicious location.

It is true that Timbuktu flourished as a trade route in many items, but surprisingly the items most traded in the Golden Age were books or manuscripts. Timbuktu could legitimately be called "booktown."

The Buktu Museum also had three-dimensional models displaying the different types of home structures described earlier. The director of the museum was a relative of the Muslim imam at the Grand Mosque. This man was very warm and friendly toward me. He was giving such welcoming vibrations that somehow I felt prompted to hug him. I asked Pastor Nouh if it would be appropriate or permissible and he smiled and nodded his approval. When I hugged him, even though I was Christian and he was Muslim, I felt a kinship; a black man from as far away as America wanted a hug.

It brought to mind Muslims who have said to me that while they and their ancestors have been Muslims for years, they didn't really believe that Islam is the answer to their spiritual problems. I remember being on a train traveling north from Delhi, India to Afghanistan and I started a conversation with two Muslims. They lowered their voices and said that they would not tell this to anyone but that they would share this with me, a black man from America. They went on to say, "We are Muslim, our families are Muslim, our ancestors were Muslim, but we do not believe that Islam is the answer to our problems. We believe that Jesus Christ is the true answer to our problems, but we will not take this from the hands of a white man." I could relate to what they were saying, given the history of our oppression by whites, but I knew that according to the Scripture, the Spirit of God uses people of any race or ethnic group to draw people to Himself.

In addition to the Buktu Museum, Jean took me to the famed Ahmed Baba Museum. In the 16th and 17th centuries (1556-1627), Ahmed Baba was Timbuktu's most renowned scholar and the museum was named for him. He wrote more than 40 books and was a brilliant teacher, philosopher and grammarian. The Ahmed Baba Institute is the only public library in Timbuktu and stores over 18,000 manuscripts. These ancient manuscripts, like those of Dr. Haidara, are displayed in cases for public viewing. The Institute's work of collecting, preserving and restoring the fragile manuscripts has been funded by several countries.

———•———

On my second trip to Timbuktu, there was more time to visit different parts of the city. I'm the type of person who likes to explore, so I expressed to Brother Nouh that I'd just like to walk around and visit certain places. Pastor Nouh was reluctant to allow me to do this for safety reasons. He did not belabor the fact, but he said that it is not really safe because as a tourist, I might be robbed, kidnapped, beat up, or taken advantage of. In my mind I was thinking that I was a pretty big man in size, 250 pounds, and my size would discourage individuals from the idea of attacking me or being aggressive toward me. Of course I knew that Pastor Nouh knew best, it was his city after all, so I knew it was wise to submit myself to his suggestions. Except for walking a short distance once or twice by myself, I was accompanied by Jean, Pastor Nouh's oldest son.

Jean and I went to different sections of Timbuktu as he pointed out certain aspects of the city and directed me to certain shops in the bazaar. Once I wanted to buy some additional recording tapes, batteries, and things of that nature. I was glad that Jean was with me at the bazaar because he could communicate for me in French, and also answer the thousands of questions I had about the bazaar, the people and the culture. Jean patiently explained things to me and it was like an education on wheels. He spoke fluent English and French as well as several Malian languages. In fact, all three of Pastor Nouh's sons are extremely intelligent and fluent in at least four languages.

Chapter Six

A Man of God
Sacrifices and Believes

After Pastor Nouh finished one of his tours, we would return to his home around three or four o'clock in the afternoon. He usually arranged his tours during the hours in which school was normally in session. Unfortunately, quite often the teachers were on strike, and this was a huge hindrance to his sons' schooling. Once we arrived at his home in the late afternoon, we would take a little rest if necessary, perhaps an hour, and Pastor Nouh's wife Fati would lovingly prepare a delicious meal. Usually we had rice, chicken, salads, hot roti (a type of flatbread), and a cup of tea. I ate my fill in the home of Brother Nouh.

One of the beautiful things I experienced about Brother Nouh and his family was his wonderful wife, Fati. She is a lovely, gracious woman and an excellent cook. She has a way of preparing fish that makes it taste unbelievably delicious. Fati has much experience preparing fish because Timbuktu is near the Niger River, where they get fresh fish, so they eat a lot of fish.

Also, she formulates some beautiful, beautiful salads from vegetables, and puts them together in a way that is creative and delicious. They also eat chicken. Another staple is rice and often the rice is prepared with vegetables. The meals were beautifully prepared and tasty. One day Fati asked me what type of fruits I like and I told her that watermelon was one of my favorites. I thought I was just mentioning this in passing, but I was humbled to be served watermelon later that day. From all indications, Fati's heart's desire was to find something to please her brother and I appreciate being ministered to by this godly woman. Fati runs her home well and is truly a blessing to Pastor Nouh and the ministry. She is exemplary in terms of her behavior as a Christian: cheerful, industrious, and faithful to her God, her husband, her children, and her community.

It is not easy being a woman running a household in Timbuktu; it is labor intensive and it makes me appreciate the conveniences we enjoy in America. Before cooking, the woman has to gather wood and build a fire; cooking is done outside in pots heated over a wood fire. As I mentioned, many have to pound grain three times a day for each meal. Most things have to be made from scratch; there are almost no processed or prepared foods in jars or cans. Washing clothes without a washing machine was another matter. Like most Malian women, Fati washes clothing with her hands in a bowl of water, in a squatting position. She takes the clothes, and beats them out on the concrete. Considering the way she did it, it was amazing how clean and bright the clothes came out. Africans like bright, colorful clothing and it is amazing how they are able to keep the colors so bright and vibrant considering how they wash them.

It occurred to me when Fati went back to Timbuktu after two and a half years in America while Pastor Nouh was getting his master's degree that she might have a difficult time readjusting to Malian life. She had gotten used to washing machines, microwave ovens, gas stoves, and vacuum cleaners. If this was so, I did not notice it when I visited the family about one year after they returned to Mali. I am sure that it must have been an adjustment, but Fati seemed to slip easily back into her Malian life.

She did have some assistance from a female relative, but from what I could tell, she did 75 percent of the work. She would get up early and I would see her sweeping the compound with a broom. She would also heat up buckets of water in the morning for Pastor Nouh and me to take our baths. Fortunately, they had running water. We would go into the bathroom, wet ourselves down, lather all over with soap, and then rinse off with the rest of the water from the bucket. Fati and Pastor Nouh did have a refrigerator, a bit old, but he had it hooked up since he had electricity in his home. He did not have a modern bathroom; the toilet was primitive, essentially a hole in the ground.

Pastor Nouh could have afforded an upgrade of his bathroom, but he was careful not to live too far above the ordinary people; he did not want to do anything that would turn the people away from the Gospel.

Pastor Nouh's home was a series of rooms arranged in a circular enclosed pattern around the yard. A small portion of the yard was concrete and the rest was sand. The floors of the rooms were concrete. Each room faced the yard and often when I came out of my room, I would sit in the yard. There was a small tree in the yard and little birds which apparently had been born in this backyard. It was quite relaxing to sit in the yard and watch the birds.

———•———

Pastor Nouh is one of the most compassionate people I have ever met. This is widely felt among his congregation, but also outside of it. One day he took me with him to do some business in the city and he met and stopped a neighbor in the street. He stopped this man and talked with him for almost an hour. I stepped aside and sat on a large rock while I waited. Once we were on our way back to his home, I asked what the discussion was about. He told me that he was trying to get the man to forgive his son. It said a lot to me that in spite of his extremely busy schedule, Pastor Nouh would stop spontaneously and try to bring about reconciliation between the man and his son. This showed his concern for people. On another occasion, while we were hosting Pastor Nouh in our home in New York, and after he had spoken at several meetings I had arranged for him, I introduced him to an African friend of mine who was also from Mali and who was living in New York at the time. Once he discovered this man needed some financial help, Pastor Nouh graciously and generously took $200 out of his pocket and gave it to him; this money was from the love gifts he had received from churches where he had spoken in America.

Another indication of Pastor Nouh's compassion and love for people was his denunciation and fierce opposition to the practice of slavery and the abuse of children by some of the tribes in the desert. From 1991 to 1996, Pastor was chairman of the Malian Human Rights Association for the region of Timbuktu. Of course his outspoken condemnation of these horrible practices increases hostility toward him, but he perseveres because of his love and compassion for the victims of these practices.

———•———

Pastor Nouh was no stranger to abuse. As an infidel in the holy city of Timbuktu, he has experienced ongoing persecution since 1967 when at the age of 15 he became a Christian after attending classes at a Bible camp held by American missionaries. His persecution was from family members, teachers, classmates, Muslim neighbors, and rebel groups. Pastor Nouh tells the story of what happened after he became a Christian:

> The Muslim priest began to shake and died a couple hours later. But before he died, he said to the people gathered around us, "Be careful how you deal with Nouh. A great Spirit lives in him and if you try to harm him, you will die as I am dying." The priest had come to our house to give my baby brother an antidote for the poisoned milk he had just tasted. Actually, the priest had given the poison to my mother to kill me, a despised Christian and an apostate from Islam in their eyes. Mother could not bear the sight of me drinking the poisoned milk, so she stepped outside leaving her baby in the room. Since I was not allowed to take my meals with the family, she had also brought my food. I thanked the Lord for the food and began to eat. My baby brother reached for the milk and drank some of it. I did not know the milk was poisoned, so I did not stop him. Instantly, the baby was paralyzed. My screams brought Mother, the neighbors and relatives. Mother's cries and screams mingled with mine as the priest came to give the child an antidote. My brother lived but was paralyzed in one leg. It was the priest himself who met an untimely death.

When Nouh was in third grade he had received a ballpoint pen from some missionaries for learning Bible verses. Some of the verses affected him deeply, but when he asked the teacher at the Koranic school about the truth of the verses, the teacher beat him and said that if he did not associate with "kafirs" (non-Muslims, unbelievers, infidels), he would not have asked such a question. Once he earned his ballpoint pen, he forgot about the troubling verses. Four years later, a missionary family offered to pay his way to a Bible camp. Nouh lied to his father, telling him it was a scout camp organized by his school. As a result of the teaching at the Bible camp, Nouh invited Jesus Christ to be his Lord and Savior and he became a born again child of God at 15 years old. A few days after he left for camp, his father was furious when he learned that Nouh had gone to a Christian camp. When he came home, his father tied him up for a week and would not give him any food to eat. He tried to pressure Nouh to renounce Christianity. After he finally let him go, he forced Nouh from his home and said, "Never come back home or I will kill you. I deny that you are my son."

Close relatives also refused to allow him to stay with them, so for two years Nouh lived with a Christian family who were formerly animists. His schoolteachers refused to correct his homework on the grounds that he was an "impure Christian." Other students would not sit with him, called him "kafir" (infidel), and Christian names such as Paul, Peter, and Jesus to emphasize his status as a Muslim "apostate." He was accused of accepting bribes from Westerners to convert to Christianity. People of his town threw stones at him. In the streets adults spat in his face, slapped him, and beat him; children threw stones at him.

After two years Nouh was allowed to go home on two conditions: that he get up each morning at daybreak, the time of Muslim prayer, and that he eat from his own dish rather than with others. A Christian suggested that he use Muslim morning prayer time for his devotional time with the Lord and he has kept that practice to this day (no matter how late he stays up, he gets up at 4:00 a.m. for his devotions). In Muslim culture, if you eat from your own dish rather than with others, you are seen as ill or impure or even a dog. This is how his family saw him when he returned.

Nouh says that it was hard to be cast aside, but it was harder for his mother. The older wives ridiculed her saying, "Are you not ashamed that your son has become the first kafir in the holy city of Timbuktu?" They made her so upset that she decided it was better for him to die than live and that is why she gave him the poisoned milk that brought such sad results.

Another instance of persecution happened in December 1995. He was almost kidnapped. Pastor Nouh said that an Arab neighbor offered to drive him to find camel's milk for a friend in Conakry, Guinea.

During the drive, Nouh became suspicious because his neighbor changed the direction of his route. Pastor Nouh then realized that this man planned to hand him over to Tuareg rebels who were upset with him for opposing their practices which included slavery and child abuse. Nouh told the man that he needed to be home immediately by 10 p.m. or else his family would call the military to say that the neighbor had kidnapped him. His neighbor was angry but turned around and drove him back to exactly where he changed his route. Pastor Nouh walked for almost two hours before getting home.

Nouh says that when he started high school, the Lord began to strongly burden his heart for fulltime Christian service. He says that he argued with the Lord, pointing out that he came from the lowest level in society, and he wondered what more people would do to him if he became God's servant. He pleaded with God to choose someone else, but the call to serve God became so strong that one day he went to see a missionary and told him what was going on. The missionary arranged for Nouh to take four years of Bible school training in neighboring Ivory Coast from 1971 to 1975.

During his vacations in Timbuktu, family members and friends tried to force him to marry a Muslim girl but he refused. He says that his wife Fati is a constant reminder to him of the goodness of God, because there were no single Christian girls in Timbuktu for him to marry. Fati heard the Gospel and came to Jesus when she was translating for a hairdresser. She too was persecuted but is a strong Christian and a great pastor's wife. Together they endeavor to serve the very community that once despised and persecuted them. Such is the grace of God.

———•———

After graduation from Bible school, Nouh worked for two years with missionaries in the area. By 1990 Nouh had led several young Muslim men to Christ and this led the Muslim community to essentially boycott their families by not talking to them or buying from them or selling to them. It was a difficult time. Their wives could not go to the market or even buy water from a faucet without problems and insults. Because he opposed some of their practices such as slavery, in June 1994, Tuareg rebels (a nomadic desert people who traditionally wear blue or indigo colored turbans and veils—they are called the "blue people of the Sahara" and are said to be the original Canaanites) surrounded Nouh's home and fired heavy guns at it while his family was doing their nightly devotions. The attack lasted about an hour and a half and the army counterattacked the rebels, using heavy tanks to drive them out of the neighborhood. Miraculously, they were spared and none of the nine family members in the home were harmed.

Nouh eventually became the pastor of the Eglise Evangelique Baptiste de Timbuktu (Evangelical Baptist Church of Timbuktu). The church grew from about 50 members in 1999 to about 205 members by March 2012. This was especially remarkable in a Muslim society where converting to Christianity means being totally cut off from family and friends and ostracized by the entire society. In a culture where family and friends are so important, it takes a lot of courage and commitment to become a Christian.

The church is involved in an aggressive kind of evangelism involving one-to-one contact. Pastor Nouh preaches two hours per week on FM radio and he has been on radio and television discussing the principle areas of contention between Christianity and Islam. Many intellectuals and youth were drawn to his weekly preaching instead of to Muslim preachers in the city. This contributed to increased hostility of Muslim imams toward Pastor Nouh. For the most part, the church has to focus their activities on Christmas and Easter as they are not allowed to do public evangelism. They use calendars with Scripture verses, the Jesus film and videos as well as distribute Bibles in French and Arabic. They also have a Women's Teaching Center where they teach women job skills which include sewing (with modern sewing machines), embroidery, knitting, dying cloth, literacy, health, and Bible class. Men are trained in mostly the same areas with the addition of driver training. The church's work is made possible through partnerships with international charities. The church has a shelter called the "Elijah House" where boys come for two meals a day. They do not stay there full time but the two meals a day make a huge difference in the lives of these boys who come from extremely poor families, many of whom subsist on about one dollar a day. Mali is the fourth poorest country in the world.

——•——

Like almost everyone else in a poor country such as Mali, Pastor Nouh and other church members were entrepreneurs. He and a friend would buy jewelry such as earrings, necklaces, bracelets, scarfs, and handcrafted items and take them to one of the leading hotels in Timbuktu and display the items for purchase by tourists. He and several of his business partners took me with them on one of these trips. From time to time, ladies would come to his home to purchase such items. Within minutes, he would lay out a beautiful display of these items. Each time Pastor Nouh visited our home in the United States, he would come bearing gifts. We received jewelry, leather pillow covers, beautiful fabric, pottery, wooden cooking utensils, tightly woven baskets, even a miniature replica of a typical Timbuktu door. Some of these items are proudly displayed on the walls in our home.

Several gifts were leather framed rectangles of the Tuareg Cross. There are 21 different designs of this cross, each representing a specific Tuareg tribe, clan or city. One of the more famous ones is the Cross of Agadez from the city of Agadez in Niger. The crosses are made of silver or nickel (it is said that the Tuareg are suspicious of gold and consider it bad luck). The cross design is said to represent the four corners of the Earth, a metaphysical and spiritual compass for a people who are always on the move such as the nomadic Tuaregs. These crosses have been made since the 16th century and some say the cross design is not in any way a symbol of the Christian religion. They are typically worn as amulets to ward off evil spirits and bad luck. Traditionally a father would transmit the cross to his son, saying, "Son, I give you the four directions as no one knows where your path will end."

There is, however, another version of the story of the crosses, according to Pastor Nouh. This version, and it is the one to which Pastor Nouh subscribes, is that the crosses have religious significance, are indeed Christian symbols, and represent an earlier experience with Christianity. The nomadic Tuaregs are descendants of Berbers, a tribe that was Christian before Islam invaded North Africa. Monica, Saint Augustine's mother, was a Christian Berber. The Tuaregs fled to sub-Saharan Africa in order to escape the sword of Islam, but they were pursued, caught and forced into Islam. However, they kept a number of Christian symbols such as the different designs of the cross. They put these cross designs on all of their belongings, including their swords, daggers, camel saddles, and leather pillow covers. These items are full of cross designs.

According to Pastor Nouh, even their Tamasheq language includes a number of words from the Hebrew and Greek languages that Christians have in their vocabularies. For example, in Hebrew, the Tamasheq called God "Messinar" (literally "our Messiah"). They called the Father "Abba" as it is in Hebrew, and the word for girl is "taliat" which is close to "talitha" the Hebrew word for girl. In the case of Greek, the Tamasheq use the word "Angellous" for angel, the same word as it is in Greek. Pastor Nouh says that his prayer is to bring back the truth of the Judeo-Christian Scriptures to the Tuareg world. Pictures of the Tuareg crosses are at the back of the book.

In addition to selling jewelry, fabric, and handcrafted items, some people scrape out a living by farming (difficult in the desert) and selling fish from the Niger River. With incomes of less than $1.00 a day, the extreme poverty makes the holistic ministry of the church crucial. Pastor Nouh's ministry is intense. His people are very needy and they come to his door often. He is continually helping, counseling, teaching, preaching, and preparing sermons. Often from early morning (as mentioned, he rises for his devotions at 4:00 a.m.) unto the evening, he is sharing and distributing grain, reading glasses and any items that come in as a result of his efforts and partnership with various mission groups.

Pastor Nouh has had the opportunity to travel and speak internationally, often focusing on contrasts between Islam and Christianity. He has travelled to England, France, Israel, Romania, the Netherlands, Cyprus, Singapore, Senegal, Niger, Central African Republic, Uganda, Kenya, and South Africa, as well as a number of times to the United States.

———•———

I feel greatly humbled and thankful to have been able to visit Timbuktu three times. This great historical and ancestral city through which hundreds of thousands of people passed continues to have a fascination for me. I deeply appreciate the work Pastor Nouh and the church are doing in order to reach the people of the Sahara with the Gospel. I am thankful to have met this great man of God who has been raised up and sent to minister in Timbuktu. Although resistant at first, Pastor Nouh embraces God's calling and is burdened with the same burden that is on God's heart. Jesus died for the people in Timbuktu and He will work mightily through the church in Mali and through those who partner with them to establish His church. He said, ". . . I will build my church; and the gates of hell shall not prevail against it" (Matthew 16:18, KJV).

Our prayer is that the work of all of the partnerships in Christ will bear abundant and lasting fruit for God's kingdom and for God's glory.

Epilogue

In 2012, six years after I left Timbuktu for the third time in 2006, the northern part of Mali fell apart. The North was overrun with rebels and Islamic jihadists. There had been unrest in this area for years but there was one factor that proved a tipping point in the situation: weapons from Libya. As Khadafy became increasingly desperate, he hired and armed mercenaries, including some from northern Mali, in order to help him fight to stay in power. After his government fell and Khadafy was killed, the weapons floodgates opened and the vast storehouses of Libyan arms were available for the taking. Rebels and jihadists, armed with sophisticated weapons from Libya easily put the Malian army—poorly equipped and no match for the rebels—on the run.

At the same time and adding to the instability, there was a coup by the Malian army in Bamako, the capital city. The rebels took advantage of the coup and the instability it caused to take over most of the North of Mali, including Timbuktu. Pastor Nouh says:

On March 28, 2012, I was warned by a relative who was a member of a rebel group called the MNLA (National Movement for the Liberation of Azawad) that if I did not leave the city of Timbuktu in 24 hours, I would be caught and killed. Therefore we fled south from Timbuktu to Bamako with the five oldest of our 11 adopted children. We also helped other Christians to escape from northern Mali. We requested, and the Evangelical Protestant Association of Churches and Missions in Mali created, a Crisis Commission to take care of the refugees from the North of Mali as they were making their way to Bamako. The Commission helps to welcome the refugees, respond to their concerns, bring awareness to donors and prioritize among future needs. Due to the imminent threat of persecution and death by the terrorist group now controlling Mali, we fled Mali for the United States in April 2012.

God's timing and His plans spared our lives as months before all this happened, we received and accepted an invitation to attend Christ Church of Oak Brook's annual missionary conference (near Chicago, Illinois). This meant that we had tickets to the United States. We flew out of our country a few weeks after the North fell to the rebels. We did what we could to help the Christians and the refugees for the few weeks we were still in Bamako, Mali. Once in the States, it was painful to hear news of the Al-Qaeda branches of Islam looting our ministries, the church's sanctuary, and our home.

Once Pastor Nouh and his wife Fati arrived in the United States, it became increasingly clear that they had barely escaped death. Not long after they arrived, his picture was circulated in a newspaper indicating that there was a bounty on his head. He was wanted by the radical Islamists by life or death; this was no doubt because of his strong Christian witness and ministry in a Muslim state. Colleagues, partners, relatives, and friends advised Pastor Nouh and Fati to stay put; eventually they applied for asylum.

The rebels and the Islamists plundered the cities in the North. There were actually several groups fighting for control in northern Mali. One group called the MNLA was the independent Tuareg (a desert tribe); they wanted the North to be a separate republic and they immediately said that the North was no longer a part of Mali, but was an independent country called the Azawad Republic. This independent country was not recognized by the international community. There was looting and sacking of all public and private money, including banks, vehicles (cars, trucks, and bikes), fuel, grain including rice and millet, laptop and desktop computers, and electronic devices. Sadly, women, even minors, were raped, often in front of their husbands and relatives and friends. Another group was the radical Islamists and Al-Qaeda branches such as the AQIM (Al-Qaeda of the Islamic Maghreb), composed mostly of Algerian radicals and Muslim terrorists; Ansar Dine from the Tuareg tribe

of the Ifoghas; and the Mujao, young West African
Muslims recruited mainly from Mauritania and
the western Sahara; and other local terrorist groups
including radical groups such as Boko Haram, the
radical group from Nigeria. They were looking to
impose Sharia (Islamic law based on what they say
the Koran, the Muslim holy book teaches) on all sub-
Saharan Africa and beyond, and not just northern
Mali. After a brief struggle, the radical Islamists took
control and immediately imposed Sharia in northern
Malian cities, including Timbuktu.

It was so painful to hear of the harsh Sharia
imposed on the people. Their version of Sharia meant
veils from the head to the ankles for women, turbans
and beards for men, no drawing of human faces or
listening to radio or music or watching television,
no playing soccer, or smoking cigarettes or drinking
alcohol. Violations of Sharia incurred heavy penalties
including public lashing; stealing led to public
amputations; they cut off hands and sometimes feet
depending on the gravity of the sin. Adultery could
lead to death by stoning. The sin of insulting their
prophet Muhammad, or blasphemy against Allah
could lead to being killed in public, sometimes by
being shot to death. Christians, who are considered
infidels, were especially targeted. Not only did
the Christians flee the radical Islamists, but many
Muslim citizens also fled in the face of such terrifying
extremism. In addition to fleeing to Bamako, some

fled to other West African countries including Niger, Burkina Faso, and Mauritania.

During the months that Sharia was in effect, many were grieved and other nations were extremely concerned about the unrest and instability in a formerly stable African state, but it was not until the rebels started moving further south and threatened the capital of Mali that the French intervened. In January 2013 French and Malian government troops retook Timbuktu from the Islamist rebels without a fight.

The radicals had fled further north a few days earlier and did some horrible damage. They set fire to the Ahmed Baba Institute which housed as many as 30,000 ancient manuscripts. This was a new building funded by South Africa. Fortunately, some sensed the danger to the manuscripts while the Islamists were in control and carefully, under cover, moved up to 28,000 of the manuscripts to safety. Even though the French intervened and drove out the main body of rebel forces from many areas of northern Mali, including Timbuktu, strong terrorist groups, suicide bombers and jihadists remain in the desert regions and even in the cities.

———•———

While in the States, Pastor Nouh has been in constant email and phone contact, helping the church in Mali. He says that the rebels are still hiding in the desert, waiting for another opportunity to attack.

Food, water, electricity, and public services are often nonexistent and are huge concerns. Death, rapes, casualties, kidnappings, and uncertainty are common, and war is a daily concern in the far North; there are various armed groups that roam the roads, threatening peaceful citizens and causing harm. They loot and sack and burn the belongings of civilians, including their vehicles, and even kill them, taking away all of their animals (their livelihood). These things are a daily reality in the northern cities of Mali.

Once it was clear that there was a bounty on his head, as refugees Pastor Nouh and Fati applied to Homeland Security for religious and political asylum, both for themselves and for their adopted children. They have been greatly helped by their prayer partners and support partners for the last two and a half years. After some friends looked into their asylum application, however, it was revealed that Homeland Security has a heavy backlog and no one can predict when Pastor Nouh's case will come up for review. Besides the safety issues, another reason Pastor Nouh tried to wait to be called by Homeland Security is because all three of his biological sons live here in the United States, as well as his four grandchildren. Returning to Mali without the interview with Homeland Security makes it very unlikely that Pastor Nouh and his wife Fati will ever be able to return to America.

However, in view of the backlog at Homeland Security and since he believes very strongly that God wanted him, despite the danger and hardship, to return home to Mali, he and his wife returned to Bamako, Mali in August 2014. They arrived safely and were met at the airport by friends and family. Fortunately, a few weeks later, they found a house which includes a guard booth to provide security. This step was taken after much prayer.

Pastor Nouh felt strongly burdened and led to return even knowing that the Islamists will keep him targeted. He also knows that he and his wife will have to start everything over from scratch and the needs will be overwhelming. For many months Pastor Nouh has received a "Macedonian call" from believers and even some unbelievers to come back to Timbuktu: "Come . . . and help us" (Acts 16:9, NKJV). He says that even Bamako, the capital in southern Mali is still unstable and dangerous. The goal is to eventually go north and return home to Timbuktu.

Pastor Nouh says that he is putting himself in the hands of God and trusting his life to Him. Many are praying much for Pastor Nouh, for Fati, and for their city. As for Timbuktu, it will take a long time to bring it back from the ruin and devastation caused by the rebel takeover.

I admire the courage of Pastor Nouh, his wife Fati, and others like them who are trickling back to rebuild their country. While the needs can seem overwhelming, there is no question but that our God is able. We know that God is with them. May His good, sweet, and perfect will be done in Mali in and through His people:

> "And we know that all things work together for good to those who love God, to those who are the called according to His purpose" (Romans 8:28, NKJV).

About the Author

Hoise Birks has a heart for missions. His commitment has always been to reach unreached people whom God loves deeply. He has been involved in hospital and prison chaplaincy in several U.S. states. His experiences include teaching, preaching, evangelism, literature distribution, church planting, and pastoring. Dr. Birks spent many years as a global missionary and is the author of *A New Man: Missionary Journeys of an African American* (HB Publishing Company, 2012). He and his wife Cynthia currently live near Atlanta in Stockbridge, Georgia and are the parents of two grown children, Daniel and Lisa.

Photo Gallery

Nomadic Family Dwelling

THE TUAREGS

Members of the nomadic Tuareg tribe -
they are called the "blue people" of the
desert because of their blue dyed clothing

Playing in the sand of the Sahara

PRAY FOR THE YATTARA FAMILY

ISRAEL NOUH JOHN FATI DANIEL

SERVING
IN
MALI,
WEST AFRICA

Pastor Nouh and his wife Fati greet some of the many visitors to their home in Timbuktu

Pastor Nouh's sons – from left: Jean Le Fe, Israel, Daniel (they are wearing t-shirts from New York)

Pastor Nouh and Hoise at the home of Pastor Nouh

Pastor Nouh sharing the Good News of the Gospel on the radio transformer in Timbuktu

Installing an electric well on the church compound

Getting water from the electric well on the church grounds

Evangelical Church of Timbuktu

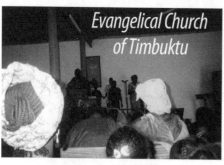

Believers worshipping in a church meeting

Church meeting – Pastor Nouh preaching

Pastor Nouh's brother Pastor Mohamed, Assistant Pastor of the Evangelical Church of Timbuktu with wife and son

Parishioners at the Evangelical Church of Timbuktu

A faithful member of Pastor Nouh's church

Visiting the Assembly of God Church

Hoise and Pastor Mohamed in front of the Assembly of God Church

Pastor Mohamed of the Assembly of God Church

Pastor Mohamed, his wife, and extended family

Water pump used by Pastor Mohamed to irrigate plots of land in the desert

Sanctuary of the Assembly of God Church

Green plants in the desert – plots of land irrigated and cultivated by Pastor Mohamed and his church members

Reaping the abundance of plants in the desert – agricultural entrepreneurs

Vegetation on plots of land (Assembly of God Church)

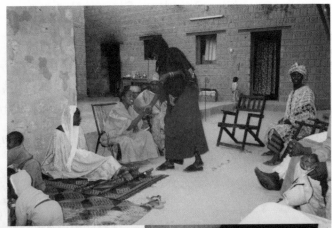

Fati with women from the church inside the home compound

Pastor Nouh and Fati with their extended family on their compound

Daniel's Bible Class (Daniel is Pastor Nouh's middle son) – his students memorized whole chapters of the Bible

Tutoring corner on the compound of Pastor Nouh's home

Students being tutored at Pastor Nouh's home

The laundry corner at Pastor Nouh's home

The Reading Glass Ministry

Pastor Nouh sorting reading glasses

Pastor Nouh making sure this man has the correct strength

Pastor Nouh having men read print to determine the strength of reading glasses

Neighbors receiving reading glasses

A man chooses from among donated pairs of reading glasses

A young lady trying on her reading glasses

Pastor Nouh's wife Fati
helping to distribute the correct strength
of reading glasses

A lady of means choosing a pair of reading glasses

A delighted young man receiving a pair of
reading glasses in Pastor Nouh's home

Pastor Nouh's wife Fati
sharing a pair of reading glasses

Women with traditional mortar and pestle help Fati prepare a meal

Pounding the grain with mortar and pestle in Fati's kitchen

The ladies say goodbye to mortar and pestle with the advent of the new Liberation Machine...

The "Liberation Machine"

Installing the Liberation Machine

Liberation Machine—a means of liberating the women from the drudgery of pounding grain three times a day with the mortar and pestle

Liberation Machine with the ground grain

Operating the Liberation Machine

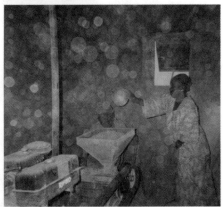

A church member putting grain in the machine

Women rejoicing outside the building housing the Liberation Machine —freed from mortar and pestle

Liberated women outside the building housing the Liberation Machine—freed from the mortar and pestle

A corner of the building – the Sankore Mosque

*The Sankore Mosque -
another angle*

The Sankore Mosque

A modern water tower

Pastor Nouh prospecting for best area to plant eucalyptus trees

Meeting with Dr. Haidara
in his home—Pastor Nouh,
Dr. Haidara (center) and Hoise

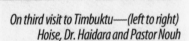

On third visit to Timbuktu—(left to right)
Hoise, Dr. Haidara and Pastor Nouh

In Dr. Haidara's home

Dr. Haidara holding an uncatalogued
manuscript in a closet at his home;
the metal trunks are full of manuscripts

*Hoise at front entrance to
Dr. Haidara's museum*

*The brilliant scholar, the Hon. Dr. Haidara
and Hoise at his museum*

*Hoise standing by display case at
Dr. Haidera's museum*

*Manuscripts
on display at
Dr. Haidara's
museum*

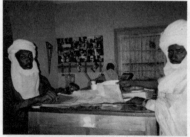

*Stylists at the Amed Baba Museum who
prepare the manuscripts for binding*

*Manuscripts on display
at Dr. Haidara's museum*

Different Home Models in the Desert

A model of a "third-class" home in the Buktu Museum

A model of a "first-class" white brick home of the wealthy – it had extra rooms for visitors

Pastor Nouh in front of a model of a nomadic home—Buktu Museum

Hoise at the Grand Mosque in Timbuktu

Students studying the Koran at the Grand Mosque

The Grand Mosque in Timbuktu is made entirely of mud

Pastor Nouh conducting a tour of the Grand Mosque in Timbuktu

Model of the old water well - like the one the city was built around

Pastor Nouh lecturing tourists at the water well (Buktu Museum)

Hoise and Pastor Nouh at the old water well (Buktu Museum)

Decorative doors, pottery, and other items on display at the Buktu Museum

Bracelets for slaves – Buktu Museum

Bottles and funnels used to store materials in the desert – Buktu Museum

Water bottles – Buktu Museum

Grains used by nomadic people for bread

Mortar and pestle – Buktu Museum

Oil lamps – Buktu Museum

Musical instruments from antiquity – Buktu Museum

A display of bowls used for cleansing by menstruating nomadic women

The Niger River

A village along the Niger River

People take small boats back and forth between Bamako and Timbuktu

Livestock being transported on the Niger River to Timbuktu

Fishing in the Niger River

Trucks and cars on the ferry to Timbuktu

Tour boat on the Niger River

Tourist boats travel between Timbuktu and Bamako when the water levels are high enough

The docks at the Niger River at Timbuktu

A tanker fuel truck being transported by ferry from Koulikoro (near Bamako) to Timbuktu

The Women's Center

Budding entrepreneur at the Women's Center

Girls learning to knit at the Women's Center

Sewing machines at the Women's Center used to teach women how to sew apparel

Women learning to knit at the Women's Center

Learning to dye fabric at the Women's Center

Young ladies from the Women's Center learning to be entrepreneurs

The Women's Center in Timbuktu

Early Scholarship

Magnified page of the manuscript

Inside of a manuscript — scholars often drew designs and wrote notes in the margins of the ancient manuscripts

Ancient manuscript from Timbuktu — these manuscripts and their contents are proof of the early scholarship in West Africa

Ancient manuscript from Timbuktu and carrying pouch for the manuscript

Tuareg Crosses in square leather frame; 21 crosses each named for different city, clan or tribe

Tuareg Crosses in octagonal leather frame

Tuareg sword and dagger in their sheaths — the handle of the swords is in shape of a cross reflecting the Christian era before the forced Islamic conversions

Tuareg sword and dagger — on the blades of the sword and dagger are three lines representing the Father, Son and Holy Spirit — a reflection of the Christian past of the Tuaregs

Church before the invasion

Church after the invasion

*Church interior
ravaged*

Also Available from Rev. Dr. Hoise Birks

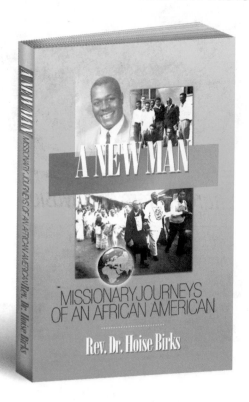

In a country where Christian commitment is often measured by getting your praise on, it is so refreshing to learn how Dr. Hoise Birks got his brave on. In this courageous response to God's call to missions, his story of taking the Gospel to the ends of the earth is as close to New Testament missions as you'll get... As African Americans we can do missions not only across the street but also and just as bibliocentric, across the seas!

Robert W. Crummie
Pastor, Mt. Calvary Missionary Baptist Church, College Park, GA
President, Carver College, Atlanta, GA